PRINCESS SOPHIA

Written by Patricia F. Martucci

Illustrated by Gayanjali Munasinghe

ISBN-13: 978-1-7355369-0-3

Dedicated to my students at The Brooklyn Charter School, who helped shape the teacher I am today. Never forget how beautiful, brave and brilliant you all are.

Love, Ms. Martucci

"Sophia, dinner is ready!

"You have to go to bed soon to get a good night's rest for your first day of school tomorrow!"

"Okay, Mommy. I forgot that a princess **NEEDS** her beauty sleep!"

Sophia carefully fluffed up her puffy dress and her curly brown hair, and took a seat at the table.

"Peas again?!" shouted Sophia. **"YUCK!"**

"You get what you get and you don't get upset!

How about we have pizza tomorrow for a back to school treat?"

"Okay," Sophia replied.

"Are you excited about school tomorrow?" Daddy asked. "Yes," Sophia said with a sigh, as she stuck one pea at a time on her fork.

"How about a bedtime story after dinner?"

"Okay!" Sophia said, with a bright big smile.

"But just one," said Daddy.

5

As Mommy cleaned up after dinner, Daddy walked with Sophia to her room.

He turned on Sophia's night light, and read her a bedtime story.

At the end of the story, Daddy kissed her on the forehead like he usually did.

"Goodnight, princess."

"Goodnight, Daddy."

As Mommy packed Sophia's lunch the next day, she called to Sophia from the kitchen.

"Come on, Sophia! I don't want you to be late for school!"

"All ready!" Sophia said, as she walked into the room, wearing an even bigger, fluffier dress than yesterday.

When Sophia got to school, she saw some of her friends from kindergarten.

"Remember to try your very best today! Try not to be nervous!" "Ok, Mommy! I love you!" shouted Sophia.

"I love you too!" Mommy replied.

As Sophia got out of the car, she carefully fluffed up her dress and her curly brown hair, fixed the straps on her book bag and walked through the front door of the school.

Some kids were getting breakfast while others were talking to their friends. Some were very excited and some looked really sleepy.

Sophia's friend from the first grade table waved at Sophia. "Hi, Luna!" Sophia said, as she walked toward her. "Whose class are you in?" asked Luna.

"Ms. Jane's class."

"Me too!" Luna said, as she hugged Sophia tight.

"Signs!" said Sophia's principal, as everyone held up two fingers, making the shape of the letter V.

Signs during breakfast meant that the kids had to stop talking because the grownups had something important to say.

"Good morning, young scholars!" said the principal. "Good morning, Mrs. Jensin," the children replied all together.

"It is so nice to see all of your beautiful faces again. We are back for another awesome school year!

By a show of hands, who thinks they remember our schools' affirmation?

Shamara, please stand!"

"I am me.

I am beautiful.

I am brave.

I am intelligent.

I am a problem solver.

And I am ready to start my day."

Everyone started clapping and smiling. It was a fun way to get everyone ready for a great day of school!

As Sophia started to walk to her first grade table, she couldn't help but to feel a weird feeling in her tummy.

Like there were butterflies in there or something! "You must be Sophia!" Ms. Jane said, with a smile.

"Yes," Sophia answered.

I'm so happy you're here! Let's start to throw away our trash and line up, following me.

Ms. Jane's class slowly started to line up. As soon as the other students in her class stopped arguing about who had spilled milk on the floor, they started to head upstairs to the classroom.

"I was a star student in kindergarten, and I'm going to be a star student in first grade," Sophia thought to herself.

As Sophia's class lined up by the classroom door, Sophia started to get that weird feeling in her tummy again.

"Good morning, beautiful first graders!"Ms.Jane said with a cheerful smile, as the children stopped at the classroom door.

"Good morning, Ms. Jane," the class responded. "When we enter the room, you'll see an area with carpet.

This is called the meeting area. Pick a spot where you think you'll feel comfortable.

"Today is Monday, September 21st, 2020. For those of you who don't know me, my name is Ms. Jane. I love to listen to all types of music, I dance, and I love animals! Let's go around the room and hear everyone's name and what you like to do for fun."

Going around the room, most answers were the same. *Fortnite*, coloring, blah, blah, blah.

"Sophia, your turn."

"I like to do princess things!" Sophia said proudly, as the class giggled.

"We don't yuck other people's yums!" Ms. Jane said in a polite but stern way.

"What are princess things?" Ms. Jane asked.

"You know, like wearing pretty fluffy dresses and stuff." "I see!" Ms. Jane said. "Well, great! Now that we have been all around the room, let's do a little review before assigning seats. Who remembers what adding is?"

"OHHHHH, I KNOW!"

"Okay, Sophia! Thanks for volunteering! What is 3+2?" "That's easy," Sophia said. "It's 6!"

"Very close, Sophia! Why don't you try using your fingers like you learned in kindergarten?"

"I don't NEED to use my fingers. It's 6."

"I'm afraid you're incorrect, Sophia. Let's count all together."

"NO! I can do it!" Sophia shouted.

"OH! Um, ok, Sophia. That's fine, you can give it another try, but please don't call out. In this class, we raise quiet hands."

Sophia was trying to count on her fingers to herself, but she was getting confused and she did not want any help from the teacher. If she needed help, Sophia thought, then she wasn't good enough to be a super star student!

"The answer is 6, Ms. Jane. I'm sure of it!"

"Sophia, 6 is not the correct answer. I'm going to let someone else give it a try, then I will show you how to add it up. Maybe you just need a little reminder."

Sophia felt upset.

"Let me get my sticks," Ms. Jane said. Ms. Jane's sticks had her students' names on them. She would close her eyes to grab one, then call on them for an answer.

"Savannah, want to try?" Ms. Jane asked. "Remember to put the number 3 in your head first."

"Threeeeee, four, five. Five is the answer!"

"Nice counting, Savannah! Did everyone see how she counted on and used her fingers to help her?"

Ms. Jane started to assign seats after the morning meeting. When everyone was sitting at their new desks, and bookbags were hung up in their proper place, she explained that the class would now be playing a scavenger hunt game to figure out where things were in the classroom.

Ms. Jane gave each group a treasure map that looked just like the classroom. She assigned each group an item to find.

Sophia's group got assigned the pencil sharpener

Sophia went up to her teacher. "Um, Ms. Jane, do I HAVE to work with my group? I can find it all by myself. I don't need help. I'm a star student."

"Yes, Sophia. You must work with your group for this activity because learning to work together as a team is an important part of first grade!"

Sophia groaned to herself, as she walked back to her group.

"Okay! Once you find your item with your group, bring it back to the meeting area all together. "Once all groups find their item, we'll go around the room and share where you found it."

Ms. Jane set her big timer and the scavenger hunt game began!

Sophia still wanted to be the first one to find her group's item. She wanted to prove to Ms. Jane she could find it all by herself.

When she began to look around the classroom she noticed that other groups around her had started to find their items. Why couldn't she?

Sophia started to feel mad.

Just then, Sophia heard a member of her group from the other side of the classroom say, "Found it!"

That mad feeling in Sophia started to get madder,

then madder,

until it was the MADDEST!

THEN BEFORE SHE KNEW IT...

Sophia was on the floor crying! She didn't know what was happening. She just knew that this feeling was way worse than the weird butterfly feeling she had had in her tummy earlier this morning.

"I was supposed to be the one to find it!

ME! I DIDN'T NEED HELP FROM ANYONE!

I'M THE STAR STUDENT! IT'S NOT FAIR!

Ms. Jane very calmly went over to Sophia and kept telling her it was okay to feel upset.

BUT IT WASN'T OKAY!

Just then, the dean, Mr. Red, happened to be passing by and heard Sophia crying. He knocked lightly on the door.

"Good morning, class," Mr. Red said, with a smile. "Good morning, Mr. Red," the class replied all together. "I think I hear an elephant in here! Is everyone okay?" Some students giggled.

"It's not funny!" yelled Sophia.

"Woah woah! The noise of an elephant is KIND OF funny.

Why don't you come with me and we can talk about what it sounds like?" Mr. Red said, smiling at Sophia.

Sophia looked at the class, then at Ms. Jane, then at Mr. Red. She slowly got up, puffed up her dress, fixed her curly brown hair, and walked toward Mr. Red.

As Sophia walked with Mr. Red to his office she thought that she was in so much trouble. "Mommy and Daddy are going to be so mad," she thought.

"So what's going on?" Mr. Red asked with a smile. Sophia just sat there and didn't answer.

"I can't help you if you don't use your words, Sophia."

After sitting silently for a bit longer, Sophia finally blurted out, "I want to go back to kindergarten!"

"Sophia, you're a big first grader now."

"I don't care. I don't want to be in first grade anymore. My class is mean. All I wanted to do was show I'm a star student!"

"I see. How were they mean?" asked Mr. Red. "Well, they, um, uhhh, they…"

"Sounds like you may be unsure of why you're feeling upset."

"I guess," Sophia whispered.

"Well, it is the first day of school, and on the first day of school, we can feel a lot of different feelings. When you let your not so nice feelings get in the way of your good feelings, you usually will have a bad day.

"How do I have a good day then?" Sophia asked.

"By being kind to your classmates and teacher. By being kind, you create feelings of happiness. That means listening to others too."

Sophia thought about that for a minute.

"First grade is going to be lots of fun," Mr. Red said. "You're not going to want to miss it just because you let those silly old not-so-nice feelings get in your way.

How about we give it another try? But this time, tell those not so nice feelings, 'Seeeeeee yaaa!

Sophia smiled. "Okay, I'll try." she whispered.

34

Sophia walked back to class with Mr. Red. She was a bit nervous the class wasn't going to like her anymore.

"Good morning again, class. Sorry for the interruption. Sophia had a little moment but she's back and ready to learn. She also has something to say."

"Um. I-uh-ummm, I'm sorry for not being nice to my classmates."

Sophia looked around the class.

"We all have those moments," said Ms. Jane.

"We're so happy you're back!"

Sophia smiled.

She took a seat right next to her friend Luna. She looked around at the rest of the class as they smiled at her and looked back at Mr. Red as he gave a wink.

This time, Sophia was ready for her first day of first grade.

Reading Comprehension Questions

1. Why do you think Sophia felt "a weird feeling in her tummy" when she was walking to her first grade table? (Page 17)

2. How did Sophia's feelings change throughout the story?

3. Why do you think Sophia had a temper tantrum?

4. What was the elephant noise that Mr. Red heard coming from Ms. Jane's classroom? (Page 32)

5. According to Mr. Red, what can Sophia do to have a good day? (Page 34)

Made in the USA
Middletown, DE
22 September 2020